That new baby will capture your heart in an instant! Why not knit a layette for that darling girl or boy, so you can lovingly wrap the wee one in softness and warmth? These four sets by Carole Prior include a hat, booties, jacket, and pants. The garment patterns are sized for six months to eighteen months. Each set is fun to knit, with its lovely texture taking shape before your eyes. So while you knit a soft layette to pamper that precious child, you can also pamper yourself with a little creativity!

Meet the Designer

"When I design layettes for babies," says Carole Prior, "I picture all of the beautiful little girls and boys who'll be wearing them. I take great pleasure in realizing that there may be thousands of small sweethearts throughout the world who are being kept warm and cozy in the designs that I've created. It's like giving a bit of myself to children everywhere."

Carole lives and works in Massachusetts as a real estate broker. She enjoys reading and gardening and loves to spend time with her husband, three grown children, and three grandchildren.

Carole says, "I was taught to knit by my mother, but it wasn't until I was married and became the mother of a beautiful little girl, Karen, that I became really serious about this very rewarding craft. I knit a pink layette for Karen and was thrilled to put it on her. I hope every child who wears these layettes is blessed with exceedingly good health and abundant happiness."

Table of Contents

LEISURE ARTS, INC.
Little Rock, Arkansas

Blue Set

▬▬▬▭ INTERMEDIATE

MATERIALS

Light Weight Yarn
 [12.30 ounces, 1256 yards
 (350 grams, 1148 meters) per skein]:
  1 skein
Straight knitting needles, sizes 4 (3.5 mm) **and**
 5 (3.75 mm) **or** sizes needed for gauge
Stitch holders - 3
Stitch markers
Tapestry needle
⅝" (16 mm) Buttons - 5 for cardigan, 1 for hat
¾" (19 mm) Elastic (for Pants) - 22{24-26}" /
 56{61-66} cm)

GAUGE: With larger size needles, in Stockinette Stitch,
  22 sts and 28 rows = 4" (10 cm)

Techniques Used:
- K2 tog *(Fig. 2, page 37)*
- Slip 1, K1, PSSO *(Fig. 1, page 37)*
- YO *(Fig. 8a, page 38)*
- P2 tog *(Fig. 4, page 37)*
- Knit Increase *(Figs. 6a & b, page 38)*

When instructed to slip a stitch, always slip as if
to **knit**.

CARDIGAN

Sizes	Finished Chest Measurement, buttoned
6 months	20" (51 cm)
12 months	21" (53.5 cm)
18 months	21½" (54.5 cm)

Size Note: Instructions are written for size 6 months,
with sizes 12, and 18 months in braces { }. Instructions
will be easier to read if you circle all the numbers
pertaining to your size. If only one number is given,
it applies to all sizes.

BACK
LOWER BAND
With smaller size needles, cast on 57{59-61} sts.

Rows 1-5: Knit across (Garter Stitch).

BODY
Change to larger size needles.

Rows 1-6: Beginning with a **knit** row, work 6 rows in
Stockinette Stitch (knit one row, purl one row).

Rows 7-9: Knit across.

Loop a short piece of yarn around any stitch to mark
Row 9 as **right** side.

Rows 10-14: Beginning with a **purl** row, work
5 rows in Stockinette Stitch.

Repeat Rows 7-14 for pattern until Back measures
approximately 7{7¾-8½}" / 18{19.5-21.5} cm from cast
on edge, ending by working a **wrong** side row.

Continued on page 4

Armhole Shaping

Rows 1 and 2: Bind off 4 sts at the beginning of the next 2 rows, knit across: 49{51-53} sts.

Work in Garter Stitch until Armholes measure 3¼{3½-3¾}" / 8.5{9-9.5} cm, ending by working a **wrong** side row.

Neck Shaping

Both sides of neck are worked at the same time using separate yarn for **each** side.

Row 1: K 15{16-17} sts, slip next 19 sts to st holder; with second yarn, knit across: 15{16-17} sts **each** side.

Row 2: Knit across; with second yarn, knit across.

Row 3 (Decrease row): Knit to within 3 sts of neck edge, K2 tog, K1; with second yarn, K1, slip 1, K1, PSSO, knit across: 14{15-16} sts **each** side.

Row 4 and 5: Repeat Rows 2 and 3: 13{14-15} sts **each** side.

Work even until Armholes measure 4{4¼-4½}" / 10{11-11.5} cm, ending by working a **wrong** side row.

Bind off all sts in **knit**.

LEFT FRONT
LOWER BAND

With smaller size needles, cast on 31{32-33} sts.

Rows 1-4: Knit across.

Row 5: K2, YO, K2 tog (buttonhole), knit across.

BODY

Change to larger size needles.

Row 1 (Right side): Knit across to last 5 sts, place marker (front band) *(see Markers, page 36)*, knit across.

Mark Row 1 as **right** side.

Row 2: K5, purl across.

Row 3: Knit across.

Rows 4-6: Repeat Rows 2 and 3 once, then repeat Row 2 once **more**.

Rows 7-9: Knit across.

Rows 10-14: Repeat Rows 2 and 3 twice, then repeat Row 2 once **more**.

Repeat Rows 7-14 for pattern until Left Front measures same as Back to Armhole Shaping, working additional buttonholes in same manner every 2{2¼-2½}" / 5{5.75-6} cm, ending by working a **wrong** side row. Last buttonhole will be in Neckband.

Armhole Shaping

Row 1: Bind off 4 sts, knit across: 27{28-29} sts.

Work in Garter Stitch until Armhole measures 2{2¼-2½}" / 5{5.75-6} cm, working additional buttonhole at established interval, ending by working a **wrong** side row.

Neck Shaping

Row 1: Knit across to last 10 sts, slip last 10 sts to st holder: 17{18-19} sts.

Row 2: Knit across.

Row 3 (Decrease row): Knit across to last 3 sts, K2 tog, K1: 16{17-18} sts.

Rows 4-9: Repeat Rows 2 and 3, 3 times: 13{14-15} sts.

Work even until Armhole measures same as Back, ending by working a **wrong** side row.

Bind off all sts in **knit**.

RIGHT FRONT
LOWER BAND
With smaller size needles, cast on 31{32-33} sts.

Rows 1-5: Knit across.

BODY
Change to larger size needles.

Row 1 (Right side): K5, place marker (front band), knit across.

Mark Row 1 as **right** side.

Row 2: Purl to marker, K5.

Row 3: Knit across.

Rows 4-6: Repeat Rows 2 and 3 once, then repeat Row 2 once **more**.

Rows 7-9: Knit across.

Rows 10-14: Repeat Rows 2 and 3 twice, then repeat Row 2 once **more**.

Repeat Rows 7-14 for pattern until Right Front measures same as Back to Armhole Shaping, ending by working a **right** side row.

Armhole Shaping
Row 1: Bind off 4 sts, knit across: 27{28-29} sts.

Work in Garter Stitch until Armhole measures 2{2¼-2½}" / 5{5.75-6} cm, ending by working a **wrong** side row.

Neck Shaping
Row 1: K 10, slip 10 sts just worked to st holder, knit across: 17{18-19} sts.

Row 2: Knit across.

Row 3 (Decrease row): K1, K2 tog, knit across: 16{17-18} sts.

Rows 4-9: Repeat Rows 2 and 3, 3 times: 13{14-15} sts.

Work even until Armhole measures same as Back, ending by working a **wrong** side row.

Bind off all sts in **knit**.

Sew shoulder seams.

SLEEVE
BODY
With **right** side facing and larger size needles, pick up 45{47-49} sts evenly spaced across armhole edge *(Fig. 9, page 39)*.

Rows 1-5: Beginning with a **purl** row, work 5 rows in Stockinette Stitch.

Rows 6-8: Knit across.

Repeat Rows 1-8 for pattern until Sleeve measures 1½" (4 cm), ending by working a **wrong** side row.

Decrease Row: K1, slip 1, K1, PSSO, knit across to last 3 sts, K2 tog, K1: 43{45-47} sts.

Continued on page 6

Maintaining pattern, continue to decrease one st at each edge, every 6{8-12} rows, 4 times **more**: 35{37-39} sts.

Work even until Sleeve measures 5$\frac{1}{2}${6$\frac{1}{2}$-8$\frac{1}{2}$}" / 14{16.5-21.5} cm, ending by working a **wrong** side row.

CUFF
Change to smaller size needles.

Row 1: Knit across decreasing 5 sts evenly spaced *(see Decreasing Evenly Across a Row, page 36)*: 30{32-34} sts.

Rows 2-6: Knit across.

Bind off all sts in **knit**.

Repeat for second Sleeve.

FINISHING
NECKBAND
With **right** side facing and smaller size needles, K 10 from Right Front st holder, pick up 14 sts evenly spaced across Right Front neck edge, K 19 from Back st holder, pick up 14 sts evenly spaced across Left Front neck edge, K 10 from Left Front st holder: 67 sts.

Row 1: K2, YO, K2 tog (buttonhole), knit across.

Rows 2-5: Knit across.

Bind off all sts in **knit**.

Sew bound off sts of underarm to side edges of Sleeve.

Weave underarm and side in one continuous seam *(Fig. 10, page 39)*.

Sew buttons to Front opposite buttonholes, making sure to sew them on firmly so baby cannot pull them off.

HAT

Size: 6 months ONLY

TOP AND SIDES
With smaller size needles, cast on 55 sts.

Rows 1-5: Knit across (Garter Stitch).

Change to larger size needles.

Rows 6-11: Beginning with a **knit** row, work 6 rows in Stockinette Stitch (knit one row, purl one row).

Rows 12-14: Knit across.

Loop a short piece of yarn around any stitch to mark Row 14 as **right** side.

Rows 15-19: Beginning with a **purl** row, work 5 rows in Stockinette Stitch.

Repeat Rows 12-19 for pattern until piece measures 3$\frac{3}{4}$" (9.5 cm) from cast on edge, ending by working pattern Row 13.

BACK
Maintain established pattern throughout.

Row 1: Work across 36 sts, K2 tog, leave remaining 17 sts unworked.

Row 2 (Decrease row): Work across 18 sts, P2 tog, leave remaining sts unworked.

Row 3 (Decrease row): Work across 18 sts, K2 tog, leave remaining sts unworked.

Rows 4-34: Repeat Rows 2 and 3, 15 times; then repeat Row 2 once **more**: 21 sts.

Row 35: K1, K2 tog 10 times: 11 sts.

Slip remaining sts to st holder.

NECKBAND

With **right** side facing and smaller size needles, pick up 20 sts evenly spaced across end of rows of Side *(Fig. 9, page 39)*, working sts from st holder, K2, (K2 tog, K1) 3 times; pick up 20 sts evenly spaced across end of rows of second Side: 48 sts.

Rows 1-5: Knit across.

Bind off all sts in **knit**.

CHIN STRAP

With **right** side facing and smaller size needles, pick up 5 sts in end of rows of Neck Band on right front corner.

Work in Garter Stitch (knit every row) for 1$\frac{1}{2}$" (4 cm).

Buttonhole Row: K2, YO, K2 tog, K1.

Last 2 Rows: Knit across.

Bind off all sts in **knit**.

Sew button to lower left corner of Neck Band.

BOOTIES (Make 2)

Size: 6 months ONLY

CUFF

With larger size needles, cast on 33 sts.

Work in Garter Stitch for 1$\frac{1}{4}$" (3 cm).

Change to smaller size needles.

Row 1: K1, (P1, K1) across.

Row 2: P1, (K1, P1) across.

Repeat Rows 1 and 2 for 1$\frac{1}{4}$" (3 cm).

INSTEP

Change to larger size needles.

Row 1 (Right side)**:** K 13, slip 13 sts just worked onto st holder, K1, (knit increase, K1) 3 times, slip last 13 sts onto second st holder: 10 sts.

Loop a short piece of yarn around any stitch to mark Row 1 as **right** side.

Work in Garter Stitch until Instep measures 1$\frac{3}{4}$" (4.5 cm), ending by working a **wrong** side row.

Slip sts to st holder; cut yarn.

SIDES

Row 1: With **right** side facing and beginning at end of row, slip 13 sts from first st holder to larger size needle, join yarn and pick up 7 sts along edge of Instep *(Fig. 9, page 39)*, K 10 from Instep st holder, pick up 7 sts along second edge of Instep, K 13 from second side st holder: 50 sts.

Rows 2-9: Knit across.

Row 10: K 20, K2 tog, K6, K2 tog, knit across: 48 sts.

SOLE

Row 1: K 27, K2 tog, leave remaining 19 sts unworked.

Rows 2-31: K7, K2 tog, leave remaining sts unworked.

Row 32: K7, K2 tog, knit across: 16 sts.

Bind off all sts in **knit**.

Sew back seam. Sew seam at back of Sole.

Continued on page 8

PANTS

Sizes	Finished Length
6 months	15" (38 cm)
12 months	17" (43 cm)
18 months	20" (51 cm)

Size Note: Instructions are written for size 6 months, with sizes 12, and 18 months in braces { }. Instructions will be easier to read if you circle all the numbers pertaining to your size. If only one number is given, it applies to all sizes.

LEG (Make 2)

With smaller size needles, cast on 50{56-60} sts.

Rows 1-5: Knit across.

Change to larger size needles.

Rows 6-11: Beginning with a **knit** row, work 6 rows in Stockinette Stitch (knit one row, purl one row).

Rows 12-14: Knit across.

Loop a short piece of yarn around any stitch to mark Row 14 as **right** side.

Rows 15-19: Beginning with a **purl** row, work 5 rows in Stockinette Stitch.

Repeat Rows 12-19 for pattern until Leg measures approximately 7{8-10}" / 18{20.5-25.5} cm from cast on edge, ending by working a **wrong** side row.

SHAPING

Maintain established pattern throughout.

Increase Row: Knit increase, knit across to last 2 sts, knit increase, K1: 52{58-62} sts.

Continue to increase one st at each edge, every other row, 3 times **more**: 58{64-68} sts.

Place a marker in each end of last row to mark end of Shaping.

Work even until piece measures $6^1/_4${$7^1/_4$-$8^1/_4$}" / 16{18.5-21} cm from marked row, ending by working a **wrong** side row.

WAISTBAND

Change to smaller size needles.
Work in K1, P1 ribbing for $1^1/_2$" (4 cm).
Bind off all sts **very loosely** in ribbing.

Weave center front and back seams from bound off edge to marked row *(Fig. 10, page 39)*.

Weave inseam.

Cut a length of elastic 1" (2.5 cm) longer than child's waist. Overlapping ends by $^1/_2$" (12 mm) and being careful not to twist, sew ends firmly together. Place elastic along **wrong** side of Waistband; fold waistband to inside around elastic and sew in place.

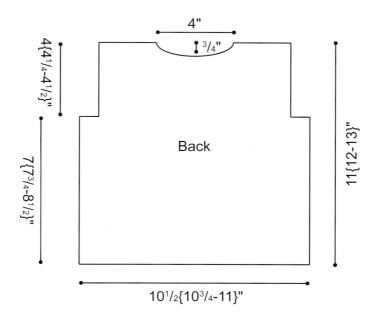

4"

³/₄"

4{4¹/₄-4¹/₂}"

7{7³/₄-8¹/₂}"

Back

11{12-13}"

10¹/₂{10³/₄-11}"

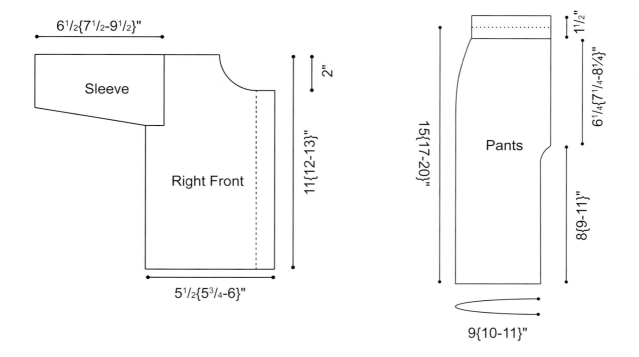

6¹/₂{7¹/₂-9¹/₂}"

Sleeve

2"

Right Front

11{12-13}"

5¹/₂{5³/₄-6}"

1¹/₂"

6¹/₄{7¹/₄-8¹/₄}"

15{17-20}"

Pants

8{9-11}"

9{10-11}"

Green Set

MATERIALS

Light Weight Yarn **3** LIGHT
[12.30 ounces, 1256 yards
(350 grams, 1148 meters) per skein]:
   1 skein
Straight knitting needles, sizes 4 (3.5 mm) **and**
   5 (3.75 mm) **or** sizes needed for gauge
Crochet hook, size D (3.25 mm)
Stitch holders - 3
Stitch markers
Tapestry needle
1/2" (12 mm) Buttons - 5
3/4" (19 mm) Elastic (for Pants) - 22{24-26}" /
   56{61-66} cm

GAUGE: With larger size needles, in pattern,
   22 sts and 40 rows = 4" (10 cm)

Gauge Swatch: 4" square (10 cm)
With larger size needles, cast on 22 sts.
Row 1 (Right side): K1, P1, (K3, P1) across.
Row 2: (K1, P3) across to last 2 sts, K1, P1.
Row 3: Purl across.
Row 4: Knit across.
Rows 5-40: Repeat Rows 1-4, 9 times.
Bind off all sts.

Techniques Used:
• Slip 1, K1, PSSO *(Fig. 1, page 37)*
• K2 tog *(Fig. 2, page 37)*
• YO *(Figs. 8a & b, page 38)*
• P2 tog *(Fig. 4, page 37)*
• Knit Increase *(Figs. 6a & b, page 38)*

When instructed to slip a stitch, always slip as if
to **knit**.

CARDIGAN

Sizes	Finished Chest Measurement, buttoned
6 months	21 3/4" (55 cm)
12 months	23 1/4" (59 cm)
18 months	24 3/4" (63 cm)

Size Note: Instructions are written for size 6 months,
with sizes 12, and 18 months in braces { }. Instructions
will be easier to read if you circle all the numbers
pertaining to your size. If only one number is given, it
applies to all sizes.

BACK
LOWER BAND

With smaller size needles, cast on 61{65-69} sts.

Rows 1-5: Knit across (Garter Stitch).

BODY

Change to larger size needles.

Row 1 (Right side): P1, (K3, P1) across.

Loop a short piece of yarn around any stitch to mark
Row 1 as **right** side.

Row 2: K1, (P3, K1) across.

Row 3: Purl across.

Row 4: Knit across.

Repeat Rows 1-4 for pattern until Back measures
approximately 7 1/4{8-8 3/4}" / 18.5{20.5-22} cm from cast
on edge, ending by working a **wrong** side row.

Continued on page 12

Armhole Shaping

Maintain established pattern throughout.

Rows 1 and 2: Bind off 4 sts at the beginning of the next 2 rows, work across: 53{57-61} sts.

Work even until Armholes measure 3¼{3½-3¾}" / 8.5{9-9.5} cm, ending by working a **wrong** side row.

Neck Shaping

Both sides of neck are worked at the same time using separate yarn for **each** side.

Row 1: Work across 16{18-20} sts, slip next 21 sts to st holder; with second yarn, work across: 16{18-20} sts **each** side.

Row 2: Work across; with second yarn, work across.

Row 3 (Decrease row): Work across to within 3 sts of neck edge, K2 tog, K1; with second yarn, K1, slip 1, K1, PSSO, work across: 15{17-19} sts **each** side.

Rows 4 and 5: Repeat Rows 2 and 3: 14{16-18} sts **each** side.

Work even until Armholes measure 4{4¼-4½}" / 10{11-11.5} cm, ending by working a **wrong** side row.

Bind off all sts in pattern.

LEFT FRONT
LOWER BAND

With smaller size needles, cast on 34{36-38} sts.

Rows 1-5: Knit across.

BODY

Change to larger size needles.

Row 1 (Right side): K0{2-0} *(see Zeros, page 36)*, P1, (K3, P1) across to last 5 sts, place marker (front band) *(see Markers, page 36)*, K2, YO, K2 tog (buttonhole), K1.

Mark Row 1 as **right** side.

Row 2: K6, (P3, K1) across to last 0{2-0} sts, P0{2-0}.

Row 3: Purl to marker, K5.

Row 4: Knit across.

Row 5: K0{2-0}, P1, (K3, P1) across to marker, K5.

Repeat Rows 2-5 for pattern until Left Front measures same as Back to Armhole Shaping, working additional buttonholes in same manner every 2{2¼-2½}" / 5{5.75-6} cm, ending by working a **wrong** side row. Last buttonhole will be in Neckband.

Armhole Shaping

Maintain established pattern throughout, working one additional buttonhole at established interval.

Row 1: Bind off 4 sts, work across: 30{32-34} sts.

Work even until Armhole measures 2{2¼-2½}" / 5{5.75-6} cm, ending by working a **wrong** side row.

Neck Shaping

Row 1: Work across to last 12 sts, slip last 12 sts to st holder: 18{20-22} sts.

Row 2: Work across.

Row 3 (Decrease row)**:** Work across to last 3 sts, K2 tog, K1: 17{19-21} sts.

Rows 4-9: Repeat Rows 2 and 3, 3 times: 14{16-18} sts.

Work even until Armhole measures same as Back, ending by working a **wrong** side row.

Bind off all sts in pattern.

RIGHT FRONT

With smaller size needles, cast on 34{36-38} sts.

Rows 1-5: Knit across.

BODY

Change to larger size needles.

Row 1 (Right side)**:** K5, place marker (front band), P1, (K3, P1) across to last 0{2-0} sts, K0{2-0}.

Mark Row 1 as **right** side.

Row 2: K0{2-0}, K1, (P3, K1) across to marker, K5.

Row 3: K5, purl across.

Row 4: Knit across.

Row 5: K5, P1, (K3, P1) across to last 0{2-0} sts, K0{2-0}.

Repeat Rows 2-5 for pattern until Right Front measures same as Back to Armhole Shaping, ending by working a **right** side row.

Armhole Shaping

Maintain established pattern throughout.

Row 1: Bind off 4 sts, work across: 30{32-34} sts.

Work even until Armhole measures 2{2$\frac{1}{4}$-2$\frac{1}{2}$}" / 5{5.75-6} cm, ending by working a **wrong** side row.

Neck Shaping

Row 1: Work across 12 sts, slip 12 sts just worked to st holder, work across: 18{20-22} sts.

Row 2: Work across.

Row 3 (Decrease row)**:** K1, slip 1, K1, PSSO, work across: 17{19-21} sts.

Rows 4-9: Repeat Rows 2 and 3, 3 times: 14{16-18} sts.

Work even until Armhole measures same as Back, ending by working a **wrong** side row.

Bind off all sts in pattern.

Sew shoulder seams.

SLEEVE
BODY

With **right** side facing and larger size needles, pick up 47{49-53} sts evenly spaced across armhole edge **(Fig. 9, page 39)**.

Beginning with a **purl** row, work in Stockinette Stitch (knit one row, purl one row) until Sleeve measures 1$\frac{1}{2}$" (4 cm), ending by working a **purl** row.

Decrease Row: K1, slip 1, K1, PSSO, knit across to last 3 sts, K2 tog, K1: 45{47-51} sts.

Continue to decrease one st at each edge, every 6{8-12} rows, 4 times **more**: 37{39-43} sts.

Work even until Sleeve measures 5$\frac{1}{2}${6$\frac{1}{2}$-8$\frac{1}{2}$}" / 14{16.5-21.5} cm, ending by working a **purl** row.

Continued on page 14

CUFF

Change to smaller size needles.

Rows 1-6: Knit across.

Bind off all sts in **knit**.

Repeat for second Sleeve.

FINISHING
NECKBAND

With **right** side facing and smaller size needles, K 12 from Right Front st holder, pick up 12 sts evenly spaced across Right Front neck edge, K 21 from Back st holder, pick up 12 sts evenly spaced across Left Front neck edge, K 12 from Left Front st holder: 69 sts.

Row 1: K2, YO, K2 tog (buttonhole), knit across.

Rows 2-5: Knit across.

Bind off all sts in **knit**.

Sew bound off sts of underarm to side edges of Sleeve.

Weave underarm and side in one continuous seam *(Fig. 10, page 39)*.

Sew buttons to Front opposite buttonholes, making sure to sew them on firmly so baby cannot pull them off.

HAT

Size: 6 months ONLY

TOP AND SIDES

With smaller size needles, cast on 61 sts.

Rows 1-6: Knit across (Garter Stitch).

Change to larger size needles.

Row 7 (Right side)**:** P1, (K3, P1) across.

Loop a short piece of yarn around any stitch to mark Row 7 as **right** side.

Row 8: K1, (P3, K1) across.

Row 9: Purl across.

Row 10: Knit across.

Repeat Rows 7-10 for pattern until piece measures 4$\frac{1}{4}$" (11 cm) from cast on edge, ending by working a **wrong** side row.

BACK

Maintain established pattern throughout.

Row 1: Work across 40 sts, K2 tog, leave remaining 19 sts unworked.

Row 2 (Decrease row)**:** Work across 20 sts, P2 tog, leave remaining sts unworked.

Row 3 (Decrease row)**:** Work across 20 sts, K2 tog, leave remaining sts unworked.

Rows 4-40: Repeat Rows 2 and 3, 18 times; then repeat Row 2 once **more**: 21 sts.

Slip remaining sts to st holder.

NECKBAND

With **right** side facing and smaller size needles, pick up 20 sts evenly spaced across end of rows of Side *(Fig. 9, page 39)*, K 21 from st holder, pick up 20 sts evenly spaced across end of rows of second Side: 61 sts.

Row 1: K 20, K2 tog 5 times, K1, K2 tog 5 times, knit across: 51 sts.

Rows 2-5: Knit across.

Bind off all sts in **knit**.

TIES

With **right** side facing and using crochet hook, join yarn with slip st in corner of Neckband *(see Basic Crochet Stitches, page 39)*; pull a 36" (91 cm) length through corner forming a double strand of yarn. With folded end around hook and using double strand, chain a 20" (51 cm) length; finish off.

Repeat for second Tie.

BOOTIES (Make 2)

Size: 6 months ONLY

CUFF

With smaller size needles, cast on 33 sts.

Rows 1-6: Knit across (Garter Stitch).

Change to larger size needles.

Row 7 (Right side): P1, (K3, P1) across.

Loop a short piece of yarn around any stitch to mark Row 7 as **right** side.

Row 8: K1, (P3, K1) across.

Row 9: Purl across.

Row 10: Knit across.

Rows 11-16: Repeat Rows 7-10 once, then repeat Rows 7 and 8 once **more**.

Change to smaller size needles.

Row 17: K1, (P1, K1) across.

Row 18: P1, (K1, P1) across.

Row 19 (Eyelet row): K1, ★ P1, YO, P2 tog, K1; repeat from ★ across.

Row 20: P1, (K1, P1) across.

Row 21: K1, (P1, K1) across.

INSTEP

Change to larger size needles.

Row 1: K 13, slip 13 sts just worked to st holder, K1, (knit increase, K1) 3 times, slip last 13 sts to st holder: 10 sts.

Work in Garter Stitch until Instep measures 1³/₄" (4.5 cm), ending by working a **wrong** side row.

Slip sts to st holder; cut yarn.

SIDES

Row 1: With **right** side facing and beginning at end of row, slip 13 sts from first st holder to larger size needle, join yarn and pick up 7 sts along edge of Instep *(Fig. 9, page 39)*, K 10 from Instep st holder, pick up 7 sts along second edge of Instep, K 13 from second side st holder: 50 sts.

Rows 2-9: Knit across.

Row 10: K 20, K2 tog, K6, K2 tog, knit across: 48 sts.

SOLE

Row 1: K 27, K2 tog, leave remaining 19 sts unworked.

Rows 2-31: K7, K2 tog, leave remaining sts unworked.

Row 32: K7, K2 tog, knit across: 16 sts.

Bind off all sts in **knit**.

Sew back seam. Sew seam at back of Sole.

TIE

Using crochet hook and double strand of yarn, chain a 20" (51 cm) length *(see Basic Crochet Stitches, page 39)*; finish off.

Weave Tie through Eyelet Row.

Continued on page 16

PANTS

Size	Finished Length
6 months	15" (38 cm)
12 months	17" (43 cm)
18 months	19" (48 cm)

Size Note: Instructions are written for size 6 months, with sizes 12, and 18 months in braces { }. Instructions will be easier to read if you circle all the numbers pertaining to your size. If only one number is given, it applies to all sizes.

LEG (Make 2)

With smaller size needles, cast on 52{58-62} sts.

Rows 1-5: Knit across (Garter Stitch).

Change to larger size needles.

Beginning with a **knit** row, work in Stockinette Stitch (knit one row, purl one row) until Leg measures approximately 7{8-10}" / 18{20.5-25.5} cm from cast on edge, ending by working a **purl** row.

SHAPING

Increase Row: Knit increase, knit across to last 2 sts, knit increase, K1: 54{60-64} sts.

Continue to increase one st at each edge, every fourth row, 2 times **more**: 58{64-68} sts.

Place a marker in each end of last row to mark end of Shaping.

Work even until piece measures $6^1/_4\{7^1/_4$-$8^1/_4\}$" / 16{18.5-21} cm from marked row, ending by working a **purl** row.

WAISTBAND

Change to smaller size needles.

Work in K1, P1 ribbing for $1^1/_2$" (4 cm).

Bind off all sts **very loosely** in ribbing.

Weave center front and back seams from bound off edge to marked row *(Fig. 10, page 39)*.

Weave inseam.

Cut a length of elastic 1" (2.5 cm) longer than child's waist. Overlapping ends by $^1/_2$" (12 mm) and being careful not to twist, sew ends firmly together. Place elastic along **wrong** side of Waistband; fold waistband to inside around elastic and sew in place.

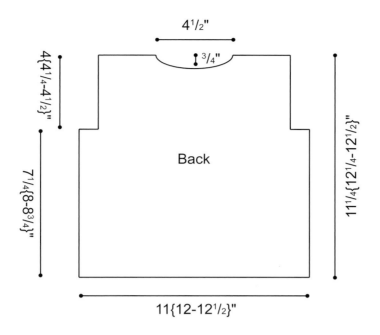

4¹/₂"

³/₄"

4{4¹/₄-4¹/₂}"

Back

11¹/₄{12¹/₄-12¹/₂}"

7¹/₄{8-8³/₄}"

11{12-12¹/₂}"

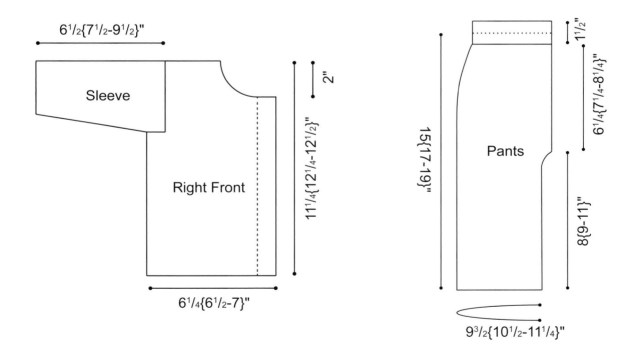

6¹/₂{7¹/₂-9¹/₂}"

Sleeve

Right Front

2"

11¹/₄{12¹/₄-12¹/₂}"

6¹/₄{6¹/₂-7}"

1¹/₂"

6¹/₄{7¹/₄-8¹/₄}"

15{17-19}"

Pants

8{9-11}"

9³/₂{10¹/₂-11¹/₄}"

Ombre Set

MATERIALS
Light Weight Yarn **3**
  [9.8 ounces, 893 yards
  (280 grams, 816 meters) per skein]:
    1 skein
Straight knitting needles, sizes 4 (3.5 mm) **and**
  5 (3.75 mm) **or** sizes needed for gauge
Stitch holders - 3
Stitch markers
Tapestry needle
$^1/_2$" (12 mm) Buttons - 5
$^5/_8$" (16 mm) wide Satin Ribbon - 2 yards (2 meters)
$^3/_4$" (19 mm) Elastic (for Pants) - 22{24-26}" /
  56{61-66} cm)

GAUGE: With larger size needles, in Stockinette Stitch,
  22 sts and 28 rows = 4" (10 cm)

Techniques Used:
- K2 tog *(Fig. 2, page 37)*
- YO *(Fig. 8a, page 38)*
- Slip 1, K1, PSSO *(Fig. 1, page 37)*
- P2 tog *(Fig. 4, page 37)*
- Purl increase *(Fig. 7, page 38)*
- P2 tog tbl *(Fig. 5, page 37)*
- Knit increase *(Figs. 6a & b, page 38)*

When instructed to slip a stitch, always slip as if
to **knit**.

CARDIGAN

Sizes	Finished Chest Measurement, buttoned
6 months	21" (53.5 cm)
12 months	22" (56 cm)
18 months	23" (58.5 cm)

Size Note: Instructions are written for size 6 months,
with sizes 12, and 18 months in braces { }. Instructions
will be easier to read if you circle all the numbers
pertaining to your size. If only one number is given,
it applies to all sizes.

BACK
LOWER BAND
With smaller size needles, cast on 71{79-79} sts.

Rows 1-5: K1, (P1, K1) across (Seed Stitch).

BODY
Row 1 (Right side)**:** K1, K2 tog, YO, K1, YO, slip 1, K1,
PSSO, ★ K3, K2 tog, YO, K1, YO, slip 1, K1, PSSO;
repeat from ★ across to last st, K1.

Loop a short piece of yarn around any stitch to mark
Row 1 as **right** side.

Row 2 AND ALL WRONG SIDE ROWS OF BODY:
Purl across.

Rows 3-6: Repeat Rows 1 and 2 twice.

Row 7: Knit across.

Row 9: K5, K2 tog, YO, K1, YO, slip 1, K1, PSSO,
★ K3, K2 tog, YO, K1, YO, slip 1, K1, PSSO; repeat
from ★ across to last 5 sts, K5.

Rows 11-14: Repeat Row 9 and 10 twice.

Row 15: Knit across.

Continued on page 20

Row 16: Purl across.

Repeat Rows 1-16 for pattern until Back measures approximately 8{9-9}" / 20.5{23-23} cm, ending by working Row 6 or Row 14.

Armhole Shaping

Row 1: Bind off 4 sts, purl across decreasing 12{16-14} sts evenly spaced *(see Decreasing Evenly Across a Row, page 36)*: 55{59-61} sts.

Row 2: Bind off 4 sts, purl across: 51{55-57} sts.

Work even in Stockinette Stitch (knit one row, purl one row) until Armholes measure 3¼{3½-3¾}" / 8{9-9.5} cm, ending by working a **purl** row.

Neck Shaping

Both sides of neck are worked at the same time, using separate yarn for **each** side.

Row 1: K 12{14-15}, K2 tog, K1, slip next 21 sts to st holder; with second yarn, K1, slip 1, K1, PSSO, knit across: 14{16-17} sts **each** side.

Row 2: Purl across; with second yarn, purl across.

Row 3 (Decrease row): Knit to within 3 sts of neck edge, K2 tog, K1; with second yarn, K1, slip 1, K1, PSSO, knit across: 13{15-16} sts **each** side.

Rows 4 and 5: Repeat Rows 2 and 3: 12{14-15} sts **each** side.

Work even until Armholes measure 4{4¼-4½}" / 10{11-11.5} cm, ending by working a **purl** row.

Bind off all sts in **knit**.

LEFT FRONT
LOWER BAND

With smaller size needles, cast on 36{44-44} sts.

Row 1: (P1, K1) across.

Row 2: (K1, P1) across.

Rows 3-5: Repeat Rows 1 and 2 once, then repeat Row 1 once **more**.

BODY

Change to larger size needles.

Row 1 (Right side): K1, K2 tog, YO, K1, YO, slip 1, K1, PSSO, ★ K3, K2 tog, YO, K1, YO, slip 1, K1, PSSO; repeat from ★ across to last 6 sts, (K1, P1) 3 times.

Mark Row 1 as **right** side.

Row 2 AND ALL WRONG SIDE ROWS OF BODY: (P1, K1) twice, purl across.

Rows 3-6: Repeat Rows 1 and 2 twice.

Row 7: Knit across to last 5 sts, P1, (K1, P1) twice.

Row 9: K5, K2 tog, YO, K1, YO, slip 1, K1, PSSO, ★ K3, K2 tog, YO, K1, YO, slip 1, K1, PSSO; repeat from ★ across to last 10 sts, K5, P1, (K1, P1) twice.

Rows 11-14: Repeat Rows 9 and 10 twice.

Row 15: Knit across to last 5 sts, P1, (K1, P1) twice.

Row 16: (P1, K1) twice, purl across.

Repeat Rows 1-16 for pattern until Left Front measures same as Back to Armhole Shaping, ending by working Row 6 or Row 14.

Armhole Shaping

Row 1: Bind off 4 sts, purl across to last 5 sts, decreasing 6{12-11} sts evenly spaced, P1, (K1, P1) twice: 26{28-29} sts.

Row 2: (P1, K1) twice, purl across.

Row 3: Knit across to last 5 sts, P1, (K1, P1) twice.

Repeat Rows 2 and 3 until Armhole measures 2{2¼-2½}" / 5{5.5-6.5} cm, ending by working a **right** side row.

Neck Shaping

Row 1: (P1, K1) twice, P6, slip 10 sts just worked to st holder, purl across: 16{18-19} sts.

Row 2 (Decrease row): Knit across to last 3 sts, K2 tog, K1: 15{17-18} sts.

Row 3: Purl across.

Repeat Rows 2 and 3, 3 times: 12{14-15} sts.

Work even in Stockinette Stitch until Armhole measures same as Back, ending by working a **purl** row.

Bind off all sts in **knit**.

RIGHT FRONT
LOWER BAND

Work same as Left Front.

BODY
Change to larger size needles.

Row 1 (Right side): (K1, P1) twice, K2, K2 tog, YO, K1, YO, slip 1, K1, PSSO, ★ K3, K2 tog, YO, K1, YO, slip 1, K1, PSSO; repeat from ★ across to last st, K1.

Mark Row 1 as **right** side.

Row 2 AND ALL WRONG SIDE ROWS OF BODY:
Purl across to last 5 sts, K1, (P1, K1) twice.

Rows 3-6: Repeat Rows 1 and 2 twice.

Row 7 (Buttonhole row): K1, P1, YO, P2 tog, knit across.

Row 9: (K1, P1) twice, K6, K2 tog, YO, K1, YO, slip 1, K1, PSSO, ★ K3, K2 tog, YO, K1, YO, slip 1, K1, PSSO; repeat from ★ across to last 5 sts, K5.

Rows 11-14: Repeat Rows 9 and 10 twice.

Row 15: (K1, P1) twice, knit across.

Row 16: Purl across to last 5 sts, K1, (P1, K1) twice.

Repeat Rows 1-16 for pattern, working additional buttonholes in same manner every 16{18-18} rows, until Right Front measures same as Back to Armhole Shaping, ending by working Row 6 or Row 14. Last buttonhole will be in Neckband.

Armhole Shaping

Row 1: K1, (P1, K1) twice, purl across decreasing 6{12-11} sts evenly spaced: 30{32-33} sts.

Row 2: Bind off 4 sts, purl across to last 5 sts, K1, (P1, K1) twice: 26{28-29} sts.

Row 3: (K1, P1) twice, knit across.

Row 4: Purl across to last 5 sts, K1, (P1, K1) twice.

Repeat Rows 3 and 4 until Armhole measures 2{2¼-2½}" / 5{5.5-6.5} cm, ending by working a **wrong** side row.

Neck Shaping

Row 1: (K1, P1) twice, K6, slip 10 sts just worked to st holder, knit across: 16{18-19} sts.

Row 2: Purl across to last 5 sts, K1, (P1, K1) twice.

Row 3 (Decrease row): K1, slip 1, K1, PSSO, knit across: 15{17-18} sts.

Repeat Rows 2 and 3, 3 times: 12{14-15} sts.

Work even in Stockinette Stitch until Armhole measures same as Back, ending by working a **purl** row.

Bind off all sts in **knit**.

Sew shoulder seams.

SLEEVE
BODY

With **right** side facing and larger size needles, pick up 41{43-47} sts evenly spaced across armhole edge **(Fig. 9, page 39)**.

Beginning with a **purl** row, work in Stockinette Stitch for 1½" (4 cm), ending by working a **purl** row.

Decrease Row: K1, slip 1, K1, PSSO, knit across to last 3 sts, K2 tog, K1: 39{41-45} sts.

Continue to decrease one st at each edge, every 6{8-12} rows, 4 times **more**: 31{33-37} sts.

Continued on page 22

Work even until Sleeve measures 6{7-9}" / 15{18-23} cm, ending by working a **purl** row.

CUFF
Change to smaller size needles.

Rows 1-5: K1, (P1, K1) across.

Bind off all sts in **knit**.

Repeat for second Sleeve.

FINISHING
NECKBAND
With **right** side facing and smaller size needles and working sts from Right Front st holder, P1, K1, YO, K2 tog, P1, K5, pick up 12 sts evenly spaced along right neck edge, K 21 from Back st holder, pick up 12 sts evenly spaced along left neck edge, working sts from Left Front st holder, K5, P1, (K1, P1) twice: 65 sts.

Rows 1-4: P1, (K1, P1) across.

Bind off all sts in **knit**.

Sew bound off sts of underarm to side edges of Sleeve.

Weave underarm and side in one continuous seam **(Fig. 10, page 39)**.

Sew buttons to Front opposite buttonholes, making sure to sew them on firmly so baby cannot pull them off.

HAT

Size: 6 months ONLY

TOP AND SIDES
With smaller size needles, cast on 55 sts.

Rows 1-5: K1, (P1, K1) across (Seed Stitch).

Change to larger size needles.

Row 6 (Right side): K1, K2 tog, YO, K1, YO, slip 1, K1, PSSO, ★ K3, K2 tog, YO, K1, YO, slip 1, K1, PSSO; repeat from ★ across to last st, K1.

Loop a short piece of yarn around any stitch to mark Row 6 as **right** side.

Row 7 AND ALL WRONG SIDE ROWS: Purl across.

Rows 8-11: Repeat Rows 6 and 7 twice.

Row 12: Knit across.

Row 14: K5, K2 tog, YO, K1, YO, slip 1, K1, PSSO, ★ K3, K2 tog, YO, K1, YO, slip 1, K1, PSSO; repeat from ★ across to last 5 sts, K5.

Rows 16-19: Repeat Rows 14 and 15 twice.

Row 20: Knit across.

Row 21: Purl across.

Repeat Rows 6-21 for pattern until piece measures 3³/₄" / 9.5 cm from cast on edge, ending by working a **purl** row.

BACK
Row 1: K 36, K2 tog, leave remaining 17 sts unworked.

Row 2 (Decrease row): P 18, P2 tog, leave remaining sts unworked.

Row 3 (Decrease row): K 18, K2 tog, leave remaining sts unworked.

Rows 4-35: Repeat Rows 2 and 3, 16 times: 20 sts.

Row 36: (P3, P2 tog) across: 16 sts.

Slip remaining sts to st holder.

NECKBAND
With **right** side facing and smaller size needles, pick up 20 sts evenly spaced across end of rows of Side **(Fig. 9, page 39)**; working sts from st holder, K7, K2 tog, K7, pick up 20 sts evenly spaced across end of rows of second Side: 55 sts.

Rows 1-5: K1, (P1, K1) across.

Bind off all sts in **knit**.

Sew ribbon ties to lower edges.

BOOTIES (Make 2)

Size: 6 months ONLY

CUFF

With smaller size needles, cast on 31 sts.

Rows 1-3: P1, (K1, P1) across (Seed Stitch).

Row 4 (Right side): K1, K2 tog, YO, K1, YO, slip 1, K1, PSSO, ★ K3, K2 tog, YO, K1, YO, slip 1, K1, PSSO; repeat from ★ across to last st, K1.

Loop a short piece of yarn around any stitch to mark Row 4 as **right** side.

Row 5 AND ALL WRONG SIDE ROWS THRU Row 17: Purl across.

Rows 6-9: Repeat Rows 4 and 5 twice.

Row 10: Knit across.

Row 12: K5, K2 tog, YO, K1, YO, slip 1, K1, PSSO, ★ K3, K2 tog, YO, K1, YO, slip 1, K1, PSSO; repeat from ★ across to last 5 sts, K5.

Rows 14-17: Repeat Rows 12 and 13 twice.

Rows 18 and 19: K1, (P1, K1) across.

Row 20 (Eyelet Row): ★ K1, P1, YO, P2 tog; repeat from ★ 6 times **more**, K1, P1, K1.

Rows 21 and 22: K1, (P1, K1) across.

INSTEP

Change to larger size needles.

Row 1: Cut yarn and slip 12 sts to st holder, re-join yarn, P1, (purl increase, p1) 3 times, slip next 12 sts to st holder: 10 sts.

Beginning with a **knit** row, work in Stockinette Stitch until Instep measures 1¼" (3 cm), ending by working a **purl** row.

Slip sts to st holder; cut yarn.

SIDES

With **right** side facing and larger size needles, K 12 from first st holder; pick up 7 sts along edge of Instep, K 10 from Instep st holder; pick up 7 sts along second edge of Instep, K 12 from second side st holder: 48 sts.

Beginning with a **purl** row, work in Stockinette Stitch until Sides measure ¾" (2 cm), ending by working a **purl** row.

SOLE

Row 1: K 19, K2 tog, K6, K2 tog, K 19: 46 sts.

Change to smaller size needles.

Row 2: P 26, P2 tog tbl, leave remaining 18 sts unworked.

Row 3: K7, K2 tog, leave remaining sts unworked.

Row 4: P7, P2 tog tbl, leave remaining sts unworked.

Rows 5-30: Repeat Rows 3 and 4, 13 times.

Row 31: K7, K2 tog, knit across: 16 sts.

Bind off all sts in **purl**.

Sew back seam. Sew seam at back of Sole.

Weave Ribbon through Eyelet Row.

Continued on page 24

PANTS

Sizes

Sizes	Finished Length
6 months	14½" (37 cm)
12 months	16½" (42 cm)
18 months	19½" (49.5 cm)

Size Note: Instructions are written for size 6 months, with sizes 12, and 18 months in braces { }. Instructions will be easier to read if you circle all the numbers pertaining to your size. If only one number is given, it applies to all sizes.

LEG (Make 2)

With smaller size needles, cast on 55{63-63} sts.

Rows 1-5: K1, (P1, K1) across.

Change to larger size needles.

Row 6 (Right side)**:** K1, K2 tog, YO, K1, YO, slip 1, K1, PSSO, ★ K3, K2 tog, YO, K1, YO, slip 1, K1, PSSO; repeat from ★ across to last st, K1.

Loop a short piece of yarn around any stitch to mark Row 6 as **right** side.

Row 7 AND ALL WRONG SIDE ROWS: Purl across.

Rows 8-11: Repeat Rows 6 and 7 twice.

Row 12: Knit across.

Row 14: K5, K2 tog, YO, K1, YO, slip 1, K1, PSSO, ★ K3, K2 tog, YO, K1, YO, slip 1, K1, PSSO; repeat from ★ across to last 5 sts, K5.

Rows 16-19: Repeat Rows 14 and 15 twice.

Row 20: Knit across decreasing 5{8-3} sts evenly spaced *(see Decreasing Evenly Across a Row, page 36)*: 50{55-60} sts.

Beginning with a **purl** row, work in Stockinette Stitch (knit one row, purl one row) until Leg measures approximately 6½{7½-9½}" / 16.5{19-24} cm from cast on edge, ending by working a **purl** row.

SHAPING

Increase Row: Knit increase, knit across to last 2 sts, knit increase, K1: 52 sts: 52{57-62} sts.

Continue to increase one st at each edge, every fourth row, 2 times **more**: 56{61-66} sts.

Place a marker in each end of last row to mark end of Shaping.

Work even in Stockinette Stitch until piece measures 6¼{7¼-8¼}" / 16{18.5-21} cm from marked row.

WAISTBAND

Change to smaller size needles.

Work in K1, P1 ribbing for 1½" (4 cm).

Bind off all sts **very loosely** in ribbing.

Weave center front and back seams from bound off edge to marked row *(Fig. 10, page 39)*.

Weave inseam.

Cut a length of elastic 1" (2.5 cm) longer than child's waist. Overlapping ends by ½" (12 mm) and being careful not to twist, sew ends firmly together. Place elastic along **wrong** side of Waistband; fold waistband to inside around elastic and sew in place.

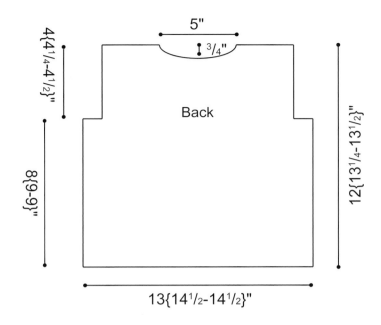

Back

5"

$3/4$"

$4\{4^{1}/_{4}-4^{1}/_{2}\}$"

$8\{9-9\}$"

$12\{13^{1}/_{4}-13^{1}/_{2}\}$"

$13\{14^{1}/_{2}-14^{1}/_{2}\}$"

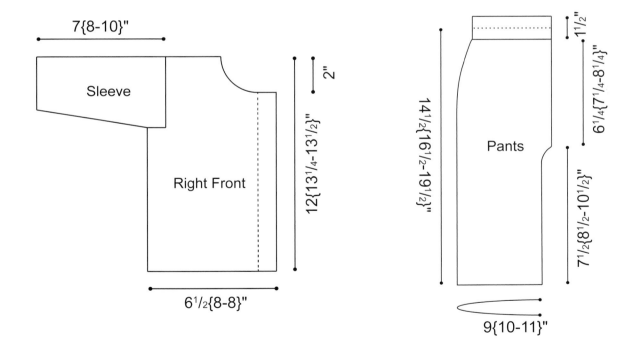

$7\{8-10\}$"

Sleeve

Right Front

2"

$12\{13^{1}/_{4}-13^{1}/_{2}\}$"

$6^{1}/_{2}\{8-8\}$"

Pants

$1^{1}/_{2}$"

$6^{1}/_{4}\{7^{1}/_{4}-8^{1}/_{4}\}$"

$14^{1}/_{2}\{16^{1}/_{2}-19^{1}/_{2}\}$"

$7^{1}/_{2}\{8^{1}/_{2}-10^{1}/_{2}\}$"

$9\{10-11\}$"

Pink Fan Set

MATERIALS
Light Weight Yarn **3** LIGHT
[12.30 ounces, 1256 yards
(350 grams, 1148 meters) per skein]:
    1 skein
Straight knitting needles, sizes 4 (3.5 mm) **and**
    5 (3.75 mm) **or** sizes needed for gauge
Stitch holders - 3
Stitch markers
Tapestry needle
$^1/_2$" (12 mm) Buttons - 5
$^5/_8$" (16 mm) wide Satin Ribbon - 30" (76 cm)
$^3/_4$" (19 mm) Elastic (for Pants) - 22{24-26}" /
    56{61-66} cm)

GAUGE: With larger size needles, in Stockinette Stitch,
        22 sts and 32 rows = 4" (10 cm)
        With larger size needles, in pattern,
        12 sts = 2$^1/_4$" (5.75 cm) and
        32 rows = 4" (10 cm)

Gauge Swatch: 4$^1/_4$" w x 4" h (11 cm x 10 cm)
With larger size needles, cast on 23 sts.
Row 1 (Right side): Knit across.
Row 2: Purl across.
Row 3: K5, K2 tog twice, (YO, K1) 4 times,
K2 tog twice, K6.
Rows 4 and 5: Knit across.
Rows 6-32: Repeat Rows 2-5, 6 times; then repeat
Rows 2-4 once **more**.
Bind off all sts in **knit**.

Techniques Used:
• K2 tog **(Fig. 2, page 37)**
• YO **(Fig. 8a, page 38)**
• Slip 1, K1, PSSO **(Fig. 1, page 37)**
• P2 tog **(Fig. 4, page 37)**
• Purl increase **(Fig. 7, page 38)**
• K3 tog **(Fig. 3, page 37)**
• Knit increase **(Figs. 6a & b, page 38)**

When instructed to slip a stitch, always slip as if
to **knit**.

CARDIGAN

Sizes	Finished Chest Measurement, buttoned
6 months	21$^3/_4$" (55 cm)
12 months	22$^1/_2$" (57 cm)
18 months	24" (61 cm)

Size Note: Instructions are written for size 6 months,
with sizes 12, and 18 months in braces { }. Instructions
will be easier to read if you circle all the numbers
pertaining to your size. If only one number is given, it
applies to all sizes.

BACK
LOWER BAND
With smaller size needles, cast on 61{63-67} sts.

Rows 1-5: Knit across (Garter Stitch).

BODY
Change to larger size needles.

Row 1 (Right side): K 14{15-17}, place marker
(see Markers, page 36), K 12, place marker, K9, place
marker, K 12, place marker, K 14{15-17}.

Loop a short piece of yarn around any stitch to mark
Row 1 as **right** side.

Row 2: Purl across.

Row 3: ★ Knit to marker, K2 tog twice, (YO, K1)
4 times, K2 tog twice; repeat from ★ once **more**,
knit across.

Rows 4 and 5: Knit across.

Repeat Rows 2-5 for pattern until Back measures
approximately 7{7$^3/_4$-8$^1/_2$}" / 18{19.5-21.5} cm from
cast on edge, ending by working a **wrong** side row.

Continued on page 28

Maintain established pattern throughout.

Rows 1 and 2: Bind off 4 sts at the beginning of the next 2 rows, work across: 53{55-59} sts.

Work even until Armholes measure 3{3$^1/_4$-3$^1/_2$}" / 7.5{8.5-9} cm, ending by working pattern Row 4.

Neck Shaping
Both sides of neck are worked at the same time using separate yarn for **each** side.

Row 1: K 17{18-20}, slip next 19 sts to st holder; with second yarn, knit across: 17{18-20} sts **each** side.

Row 2: Purl across; with second yarn, purl across.

Row 3: K 11{12-14}, K2 tog, YO, K1, K2 tog, K1; with second yarn, K1, slip 1, K1, PSSO, YO, K1, K2 tog, knit across: 16{17-19} sts **each** side.

Row 4: Knit across; with second yarn, knit across.

Row 5 (Decrease row)**:** Knit across to within 3 sts of neck edge, K2 tog, K1; with second yarn, K1, slip 1, K1, PSSO, knit across: 15{16-18} sts **each** side.

Row 6: Purl across; with second yarn, purl across.

Row 7: Repeat Row 5: 14{15-17} sts **each** side.

Row 8: Knit across; with second yarn, knit across.

Bind off all sts in **knit**.

LEFT FRONT
LOWER BAND
With smaller size needles, cast on 33{34-36} sts.

Rows 1-5: Knit across.

BODY
Change to larger size needles.

Row 1 (Right side)**:** K 14{15-17}, place marker, K 12, place marker, K7.

Mark Row 1 as **right** side.

Row 2: K5 (front band), place marker, purl across.

Row 3: Knit to marker, K2 tog twice, (YO, K1) 4 times, K2 tog twice, knit across.

Rows 4 and 5: Knit across.

Repeat Rows 2-5 for pattern until Left Front measures same as Back to Armhole Shaping, ending by working a **wrong** side row.

Armhole Shaping
Maintain established pattern throughout.

Row 1: Bind off 4 sts, work across: 29{30-32} sts.

Work even until Armhole measures 2{2$^1/_4$-2$^1/_2$}" / 5{5.75-6} cm, ending by working pattern Row 4.

Neck Shaping
Row 1: Knit across to last 10 sts, slip last 10 sts to st holder: 19{20-22} sts.

Row 2: Purl across.

Row 3 (Decrease row)**:** Knit to marker, K2 tog twice, (YO, K1) twice, K2 tog, K1: 18{19-21} sts.

Row 4: Knit across.

Row 5 (Decrease row)**:** Knit across to last 3 sts, K2 tog, K1: 17{18-20} sts.

Row 6: Purl across.

Row 7: Knit to marker, K2 tog, YO, K1, K2 tog, K1: 16{17-19} sts.

Row 8: Knit across.

Rows 9 and 10: Repeat Rows 5 and 6 once, then repeat Row 5 once **more**: 14{15-17} sts.

Work even until Armhole measures same as Back, ending by working pattern Row 4.

Bind off all sts in **knit**.

RIGHT FRONT
LOWER BAND
With smaller size needles, cast on 33{34-36} sts.

Rows 1-5: Knit across.

BODY
Change to larger size needles.

Row 1 (Right side)**:** K2, YO, K2 tog (buttonhole), K3, K 12, place marker, K 14{15-17}.

Row 2: Purl across to last 5 sts, place marker, K5 (front band).

Row 3: Knit to second marker, K2 tog twice, (YO, K1) 4 times, K2 tog twice, knit across.

Rows 4 and 5: Knit across.

Repeat Rows 2-5 for pattern until Right Front measures same as Back to Armhole Shaping, working additional buttonholes in same manner every 2{2¼-2½}" / 5{5.75-6} cm, ending by working a **right** side row. Last buttonhole will be in Neckband.

Armhole Shaping
Maintain established pattern throughout.

Row 1: Bind off 4 sts, work across: 29{30-32} sts.

Work even until Armholes measure 2{2¼-2½}" / 5{5.75-6} cm, ending by working pattern Row 4.

Neck Shaping
Row 1: K 10, slip 10 sts just worked to st holder, knit across: 19{20-22} sts.

Row 2: Purl across.

Row 3 (Decrease row)**:** K1, slip 1, K1, PSSO, (YO, K1) twice,
K2 tog twice, knit across: 18{19-21} sts.

Row 4: Knit across.

Row 5 (Decrease row)**:** K1, slip 1, K1, PSSO, knit across: 17{18-20} sts.

Row 6: Purl across.

Row 7: K1, K2 tog, K1, YO, K1, K2 tog, knit across: 16{17-19} sts.

Row 8: Knit across.

Rows 9-11: Repeat Rows 5 and 6 once, then repeat Row 5 once **more**: 14{15-17} sts.

Work even until Right Front measures same as Back, ending by working pattern Row 4.

Bind off all sts in **knit**.

Sew shoulder seams.

SLEEVE
BODY
With **right** side facing and larger size needles, pick up 47{49-53} sts evenly spaced across armhole edge **(Fig. 9, page 39)**.

Row 1: P7{8-10}, place marker, P 12, place marker, P9, place marker, P 12, place marker, P7{8-10}.

Row 2: ★ Knit to marker, K2 tog twice, (YO, K1) 4 times, K2 tog twice; repeat from ★ once **more**, knit across.

Rows 3 and 4: Knit across.

Row 5: Purl across.

Repeating Rows 2-5 for pattern until Sleeve measures 1½" (4 cm), ending by working pattern Row 3.

Decrease Row: K1, slip 1, K1, PSSO, knit across to last 3 sts, K2 tog, K1: 45{47-51} sts.

Continue to decrease one st at each edge, every 8{10-12} rows, 4 times **more**: 37{39-43} sts.

Work even until Sleeve measures 5½{6½-8½}" / 14{16.5-21.5} cm, ending by working pattern Row 4.

Continued on page 30

CUFF

Change to smaller size needles.

Rows 1-5: Knit across.

Bind off all sts in **knit**.

Repeat for second Sleeve.

FINISHING
NECKBAND

With **right** side facing and smaller size needles, K 10 from Right Front st holder, pick up 14 sts evenly spaced across Right Front neck edge, K 19 from Back st holder, pick up 14 sts evenly spaced across Left Front neck edge, K 10 from Left Front st holder: 67 sts.

Row 1: Knit across to last 4 sts, K2 tog, YO (buttonhole), K2.

Rows 2-5: Knit across.

Bind off all sts in **knit**.

Sew bound off sts of underarm to side edges of Sleeve.

Weave underarm and side in one continuous seam *(Fig. 10, page 39)*.

Sew buttons to Front opposite buttonholes, making sure to sew them on firmly so baby cannot pull them off.

HAT

Size: 6 months ONLY

TOP AND SIDES

With smaller size needles, cast on 54 sts.

Rows 1-5: Knit across (Garter Stitch).

Change to larger size needles.

Row 6 (Right side): K2, place marker *(see Markers, page 36)*, K 12, place marker, ★ K7, place marker, K 12, place marker; repeat from ★ once **more**,

K2. Loop a short piece of yarn around any stitch to mark Row 6 as **right** side.

Row 7: Purl across.

Row 8: ★ Knit to marker, K2 tog twice, (YO, K1) 4 times, K2 tog twice; repeat from ★ 2 times **more**, knit across.

Rows 9 and 10: Knit across.

Repeat Rows 7-10 for pattern until piece measures 3³/₄" (9.5 cm), ending by working pattern Row 9.

BACK

Row 1: K 36, K2 tog, leave remaining 16 sts unworked.

Row 2 (Decrease row): Work across 19 sts, P2 tog, leave remaining sts unworked.

Row 3 (Decrease row): Work across 19 sts, K2 tog, leave remaining sts unworked.

Rows 4-31: Repeat Rows 2 and 3, 14 times.

Row 32: Work across 19 sts, P2 tog, purl across: 22 sts.

Row 33: K1, (K2 tog, K1) across: 15 sts.

Slip remaining sts to st holder.

NECKBAND

With **right** side facing and smaller size needles, pick up 20 sts evenly spaced across end of rows of Side; working sts from st holder, (K2 tog, K1) 5 times, pick up 20 sts evenly spaced across end of rows of second Side: 50 sts.

Row 1: Knit across.

Row 2: K 23, K2 tog twice, knit across: 48 sts.

Rows 3-5: Knit across.

Bind off all sts in **knit**.

Sew ribbon ties to lower edges.

BOOTIES (Make 2)

Size: 6 months ONLY

CUFF

With smaller size needles, cast on 36 sts.

Rows 1-5: Knit across (Garter Stitch).

Change to larger size needles.

Row 6 (Right side)**:** K 12, ★ place marker **(see Markers, page 36)**, K 12; repeat from ★ once **more**.

Loop a short piece of yarn around any stitch to mark Row 6 as **right** side.

Row 7: Purl across.

Row 8: Knit to marker, K2 tog twice, (YO, K1) 4 times, K2 tog twice, knit across.

Rows 9 and 10: Knit across.

Rows 11-13: Repeat Rows 7-9.

Change to smaller size needles.

Work 7 rows in K1, P1 ribbing.

INSTEP

Row 1: P1, purl increase, P 10, slip 13 sts just worked to st holder, P 12, slip last 12 sts to st holder: 12 sts.

Row 2: K2 tog twice, (YO, K1) 4 times, K2 tog twice.

Rows 3 and 4: Knit across.

Row 5: Purl across.

Rows 6-17: Repeat Rows 2-5, 3 times.

Slip sts to st holder; cut yarn.

SIDES

Row 1: With **wrong** side facing and beginning at end of row, slip 12 sts from side st holder to larger size needle, P 10, purl increase, P1: 13 sts.

Row 2: K 13, pick up 7 sts along edge of Instep, K 12 from Instep st holder; pick up 7 sts along second edge of Instep, K 13 from last st holder: 52 sts.

Row 3: Purl across.

Row 4: K 20, K2 tog twice, (YO, K1) 4 times, K2 tog twice, knit across.

Row 5: Knit across.

SOLE

Row 1: K 18, K2 tog, K 12, K2 tog, knit across: 50 sts.

Row 2: P 30, P2 tog, leave remaining 18 sts unworked.

Row 3: K2 tog twice, (YO, K1) 4 times, K2 tog, K3 tog, leave remaining sts unworked.

Rows 4 and 5: K 11, K2 tog, leave remaining sts unworked.

Row 6: P 11, P2 tog, leave remaining sts unworked.

Rows 7-30: Repeat Rows 3-6, 6 times: 21 sts.

Row 31: K2 tog twice, (YO, K1) 4 times, K2 tog, K3 tog, knit across: 20 sts.

Bind off all sts in **knit**.

Sew back seam. Sew seam at back of Sole.

Continued on page 32

PANTS

Sizes

Sizes	Finished Length
6 months	15¼" (38.5 cm)
12 months	18¼" (46.5 cm)
18 months	20¼" (51.5 cm)

Size Note: Instructions are written for size 6 months, with sizes 12, and 18 months in braces { }. Instructions will be easier to read if you circle all the numbers pertaining to your size. If only one number is given, it applies to all sizes.

LEG (Make 2)

With smaller size needles, cast on 54{58-62} sts.

Rows 1-5: Knit across (Garter Stitch).

Change to larger size needles.

Row 6 (Right side)**:** K 21{23-25}, place marker **(see Markers, page 36)**, K 12, place marker, knit across.

Loop a short piece of yarn around any stitch to mark Row 6 as **right** side.

Row 7: Purl across.

Row 8: Knit to marker, K2 tog twice, (YO, K1) 4 times, K2 tog twice, knit across.

Rows 9 and 10: Knit across.

Repeat Rows 7-10 for pattern until Leg measures approximately 7¼{9¼-10¼}" / 18.5{23.5-26} cm from cast on edge, ending by working pattern Row 7.

SHAPING

Maintain established pattern throughout.

Increase Row: Knit increase, knit across to last 2 sts, knit increase, K1: 56{60-64} sts.

Continue to increase one st at each edge, every fourth row, 2 times **more**: 60{64-68} sts.

Place a marker in each end of last row to mark end of Shaping.

Work even until piece measures 6¼{7¼-8¼}" / 16{18.5-21} cm from marked row, ending by working pattern Row 9.

WAISTBAND

Change to smaller size needles.

Work in K1, P1 ribbing for 1½" (4 cm).

Bind off **very loosely** in ribbing.

Weave center front and back seams from bound off edge to marked row **(Fig. 10, page 39)**.

Weave inseam.

Cut a length of elastic 1" (2.5 cm) longer than child's waist. Overlapping ends by ½" (12 mm) and being careful not to twist, sew ends firmly together. Place elastic along **wrong** side of Waistband; fold waistband to inside around elastic and sew in place.

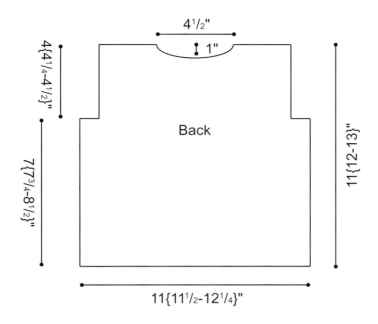

4¹/₂"

1"

4{4¹/₄-4¹/₂}"

7{7³/₄-8¹/₂}"

Back

11{12-13}"

11{11¹/₂-12¹/₄}"

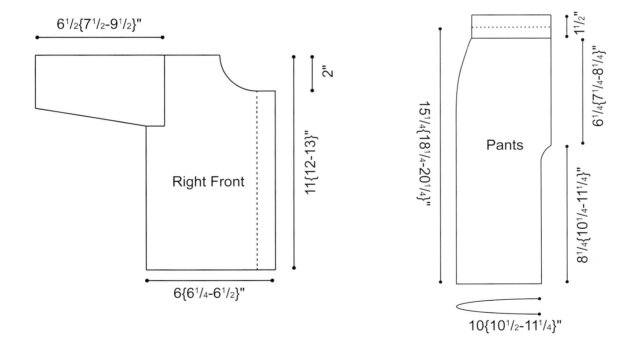

6¹/₂{7¹/₂-9¹/₂}"

2"

Right Front

11{12-13}"

6{6¹/₄-6¹/₂}"

1¹/₂"

15¹/₄{18¹/₄-20¹/₄}"

6¹/₄{7¹/₄-8¹/₄}"

Pants

8¹/₄{10¹/₄-11¹/₄}"

10{10¹/₂-11¹/₄}"

General Instructions

ABBREVIATIONS

cm	centimeters
K	knit
mm	millimeters
P	purl
PSSO	pass slipped stitch over
st(s)	stitch(es)
tbl	through back loop(s)
tog	together
YO	yarn over

★ — work instructions following ★ as many **more** times as indicated in addition to the first time.

( ) or [ ] — work enclosed instructions as many times as specified by the number immediately following **or** contains explanatory remarks.

colon (:) — the numbers given after a colon at the end of a row or round denote the number of stitches you should have on that row or round.

work even — work without increasing or decreasing in the established pattern

Yarn Weight Symbol & Names	LACE 0	SUPER FINE 1	FINE 2	LIGHT 3	MEDIUM 4	BULKY 5	SUPER BULKY 6
Type of Yarns in Category	Fingering, size 10 crochet thread	Sock, Fingering, Baby	Sport, Baby	DK, Light Worsted	Worsted, Afghan, Aran	Chunky, Craft, Rug	Bulky, Roving
Knit Gauge Range* in Stockinette St to 4" (10 cm)	33-40** sts	27-32 sts	23-26 sts	21-24 sts	16-20 sts	12-15 sts	6-11 sts
Advised Needle Size Range	000-1	1 to 3	3 to 5	5 to 7	7 to 9	9 to 11	11 and larger

*GUIDELINES ONLY: The chart above reflects the most commonly used gauges and needle sizes for specific yarn categories.

** Lace weight yarns are usually knitted on larger needles to create lacy openwork patterns. Accordingly, a gauge range is difficult to determine. Always follow the gauge stated in your pattern.

KNIT TERMINOLOGY

UNITED STATES		INTERNATIONAL
gauge	=	tension
bind off	=	cast off
yarn over (YO)	=	yarn forward (yfwd) **or**
		yarn around needle (yrn)

KNITTING NEEDLES

U.S.	0	1	2	3	4	5	6	7	8	9	10	10½	11	13	15	17
U.K.	13	12	11	10	9	8	7	6	5	4	3	2	1	00	000	---
Metric - mm	2	2.25	2.75	3.25	3.5	3.75	4	4.5	5	5.5	6	6.5	8	9	10	12.75

▰▱▱▱ **BEGINNER**	Projects for first-time knitters using basic knit and purl stitches. Minimal shaping.
▰▰▱▱ **EASY**	Projects using basic stitches, repetitive stitch patterns, simple color changes, and simple shaping and finishing.
▰▰▰▱ **INTERMEDIATE**	Projects with a variety of stitches, such as basic cables and lace, simple intarsia, double-pointed needles and knitting in the round needle techniques, mid-level shaping and finishing.
▰▰▰▰ **EXPERIENCED**	Projects using advanced techniques and stitches, such as short rows, fair isle, more intricate intarsia, cables, lace patterns, and numerous color changes.

GAUGE

Exact gauge is **essential** for proper size. Before beginning your project, make a sample swatch in the yarn and needle specified in the individual instructions. After completing the swatch, measure it, counting your stitches and rows carefully. If your swatch is larger or smaller than specified, **make another, changing needle size to get the correct gauge**. Keep trying until you find the size needles that will give you the specified gauge. Once proper gauge is obtained, measure width of piece approximately every 3" (7.5 cm) to be sure gauge remains consistent.

MARKERS

As a convenience to you, we have used markers to help distinguish the beginning of a pattern. Place markers as instructed. You may use purchased markers or tie a length of contrasting color yarn around the needle. When you reach a marker on each row, slip it from the left needle to the right needle; remove it when no longer needed.

ZEROS

To consolidate the length of an involved pattern, Zeros are sometimes used so that all sizes can be combined. For example, increase every sixth row 5{1-0} time(s) means the first size would increase 5 times, the second size would increase once, and the largest size would do nothing.

DECREASING EVENLY ACROSS A ROW

Add one to the number of decreases required and divide that number into the number of stitches on the needle. (If it is not a whole number, round up). Subtract 2 from the result and the new number is the number of stitches to be worked **between** each decrease.

Sometimes you will need to work fewer stitches between the decreases to arrive at the correct total number of stitches. Remember, the point is to reach that total with the decreases spaced out as evenly as possible.

EXAMPLE

60 stitches to be decreased by 6 evenly = total 54
6 + 1 = 7
60 ÷ 7 = 9 **(rounded up)**
9 - 2 = 7
Work 7 stitches between decreases (space stitches)

7 x 7 = 49 space stitches
    + 6 decrease stitches
    55 **total**

Since 54 is the goal, eliminate the one extra space stitch in the center, like this:

$$7 \cdot 7 \cdot 7 \cdot 6 \cdot 7 \cdot 7 \cdot 7$$
(54 stitches total)
• = decrease stitch = 1 stitch

DECREASES
SLIP 1, KNIT 1, PASS SLIPPED STITCH OVER

(abbreviated slip 1, K1, PSSO)

Slip one stitch as if to **knit**. Knit the next stitch. With the left needle, bring the slipped stitch over the knit stitch **(Fig. 1)** and off the needle.

Fig. 1

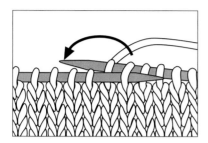

KNIT 2 TOGETHER

(abbreviated K2 tog)

Insert the right needle into the **front** of the first two stitches on the left needle as if to **knit (Fig. 2)**, then knit them together as if they were one stitch.

Fig. 2

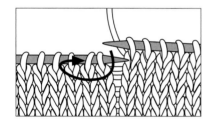

KNIT 3 TOGETHER

(abbreviated K3 tog)

Insert the right needle into the **front** of the first three stitches on the left needle as if to **knit (Fig. 3)**, then knit them together as if they were one stitch.

Fig. 3

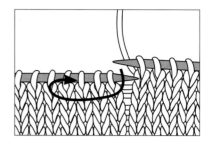

PURL 2 TOGETHER

(abbreviated P2 tog)

Insert the right needle into the **front** of the first two stitches on the left needle as if to **purl (Fig. 4)**, then purl them together as if they were one stitch.

Fig. 4

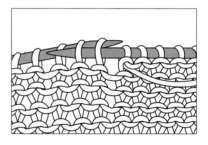

PURL 2 TOGETHER THROUGH THE BACK LOOP

(abbreviated P2 tog tbl)

Insert the right needle from **left** to **right** into the second stitch, then the first stitch on the left needle **(Fig. 5)**, then purl them together as if they were one stitch.

Fig. 5

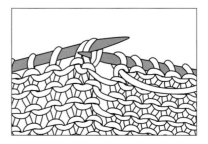

INCREASES
KNIT INCREASE

Knit the next stitch but do **not** slip the old stitch off the left needle *(Fig. 6a)*. Insert the right needle into the **back** loop of the **same** stitch and knit it *(Fig. 6b)*, then slip the old stitch off the left needle.

Fig. 6a

Fig. 6b

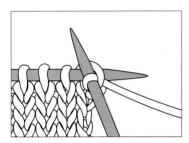 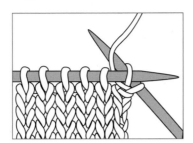

PURL INCREASE

Purl the next stitch but do **not** slip the old stitch off the left needle. Insert the right needle into the **back** loop of the **same** stitch from **back** to **front** *(Fig. 7)* and purl it. Slip the old stitch off the left needle.

Fig. 7

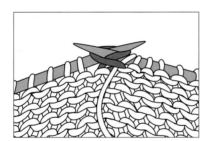

YARN OVERS *(abbreviated YO)*

After a knit stitch, before a knit stitch

Bring the yarn forward **between** the needles, then back **over** the top of the right hand needle, so that it is now in position to knit the next stitch *(Fig. 8a)*.

After a purl stitch, before a purl stitch

Take yarn **over** the right hand needle to the back, then forward under it, so that it is now in position to purl the next stitch *(Fig. 8b)*.

Fig. 8a   **Fig. 8b**

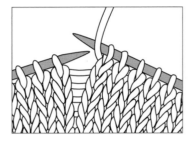 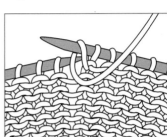